Baseball's SLUGGERS AND PITCHERS

By Steve Buckley

CONTENTS

Greg Maddux's stellar pitching earned him four Cy Young Awards.

Introduction

Whenever a slugger steps up to the plate, he has to wonder what he'll face from a pitcher. Will it be a blazing fastball? A slider? A cutter? Will he be able to blast a monster home run or get a base hit, or will he strike out?

Sluggers do their best to conquer pitchers by getting a hit. Pitchers try to keep sluggers hitless. Watching that battle between sluggers and pitchers is what makes baseball exciting.

In SPORTS ILLUSTRATED FOR KIDS *Baseball's Slugger and Pitchers,* we've profiled 14 of the major league's hottest stars. You'll read about aces such as Pedro Martinez, Roger Clemens, and Greg Maddux, who can be counted on to win big games. You will learn how Curt Schilling and Randy Johnson struggled to become stars.

Then there's Mark McGwire and Slammin' Sammy Sosa. You will read about this amazing duo's history-making year of 1998. And don't forget Ken Griffey, Junior: He may be young, but he has already piled up quite a few baseball records.

The players in *Sluggers and Pitchers* are the very best in baseball today. Some are future Hall of Famers. How did they get there and what makes them so great?

You'll be surprised at some of the things they say about their jobs *and* one another. So what are you waiting for? Turn the page and enjoy!

SAMMY SOSA

Rightfielder, Chicago Cubs

In 1998, Sammy helped lead the Cubs to the playoffs for the first time since 1989.

Sammy Sosa broke into the major leagues with the Texas Rangers in 1989. He was only 20 years old. In 25 games with the Rangers, Sammy hit just one home run. It was a home run he will never forget. "When I hit that ball, I knew I belonged in the big leagues," says Sammy.

Of course, most baseball fans remember the home runs Sammy hit in 1998. That's when he traded homers with the St. Louis Cardinals' Mark McGwire in the greatest long-ball race in baseball history. But it took Sammy a long time to become a super slugger.

Texas traded Sammy to the Chicago White Sox before the 1989 season was even over. The White Sox sent him back to the minor leagues. Sammy bounced back and forth to the minors for two seasons with the Sox. Then, after the 1991 season, Sammy was traded to the Chicago Cubs. He was thrilled!

After joining the Cubs, Sammy turned into one of the best home-run hitters in baseball. What happened? He spent a lot of time working on his hitting.

By 1998, Sammy was ready to make history. When Mark started to challenge the record for most home runs in a single season, Sammy joined right in. Mark broke Roger Maris's 37-year-old record of 61 home runs first and finished the season with 70 homers. But Sammy also passed Roger's record and hit 66 home runs!

When the 1999 season began, Sammy was ready to go again. In September, Slammin' Sammy became the first player to hit 60 home runs two seasons in a row.

"Sammy isn't just a great hitter. He always plays with a smile." — Mark Grace, Chicago Cub first baseman

SAMMY FACTS

BORN: November 12, 1968, in San Pedro de Macoris, Dominican Republic
HEIGHT: 6'
WEIGHT: 210 pounds
ENTERED MAJORS: 1989

CAREER HIGHLIGHTS

• Smashed 66 home runs in 1998, the second-highest total in baseball history
• Became the fastest player to reach 50 homers in a season (121 games), in 1998
• Was named the National League MVP in 1998.

"Greg is better than most pitchers because he's smarter."
— Tony Gwynn, San Diego Padre outfielder

PAUL JASIENSKI

Greg knows how to keep batters guessing.

MADDUX

Pitcher, Atlanta Braves

GREG FACTS

Born: April 14, 1966, in San Angelo, Texas
Height: 6'
Weight: 185 pounds
Entered Majors: 1986

CAREER HIGHLIGHTS

• Won the National League's Cy Young Award four seasons in a row (1992-1995)
• Pitched against his older brother, Mike, on September 29, 1986. Greg's Chicago Cubs beat Mike's Philadelphia Phillies, 8–3.

Atlanta Brave pitcher Greg Maddux does not throw as hard as a lot of other pitchers. He is not big, and he does not look nearly as terrifying as Randy Johnson of the Arizona Diamondbacks and Roger Clemens of the New York Yankees. But for much of the 1990's, Greg has been as good, or better, than any of them.

Why is Greg so good? Because he fools hitters. Greg uses his head and the tools he has to out-smart his opponents. He constantly changes the speed of his pitches to keep hitters off-balance. He specializes in knowing what pitch the batter is expecting. Then he throws a *different* pitch.

"To be a good pitcher, you have to think like a hitter," Greg says. "Why do you think I sit beside our hitting coach every game when I'm not pitching? It's not because I like him so much."

Another key to Greg's success is the out-standing control he has of his pitches. He can usually throw the ball to exactly where his catcher holds his mitt.

"He throws a ball that looks like it's going to be a foot and a half outside, and then it breaks back over the corner with pinpoint accuracy," says Baltimore Oriole first baseman Jeff Conine.

From late in the 1991 season until 1998, Greg had a remarkable 126–49 record with a 2.05 earned-run average. He *always* keeps looking for new ways to improve his pitching. Every day, he talks with Leo Mazzone, his pitching coach on the Braves, to get advice. Greg also looks at videotapes of his pitching performances to find mistakes.

"He has one of the brightest pitching minds I've ever been around," says Coach Mazzone, "including most coaches."

That bright mind creates a lot of *dark* days for opposing batters!

DEREK JETER

Shortstop, New York Yankees

With his fancy fielding and booming bat, Derek Jeter of the New York Yankees is becoming one of the best all-around players in the major leagues.

Derek can hit for average and for power. He can steal bases. And he can make the toughest fielding plays look easy.

In 1996, Derek became the first rookie to start at shortstop for the Yankees in 34 years. He batted .314 and was named American League Rookie of the Year. The Yankees won the World Series.

In his first three seasons (1996-98), Derek averaged .308, with 39 home runs and 332 RBIs. He ended the 1998 regular season batting .324, and the Yankees were world champions again! In 1999, Derek reached career highs in home runs and RBIs.

In the field, Derek has great range and a strong, accurate arm. He will go deep into the hole between shortstop and third base to turn sure-fire base hits into outs.

Fans are always arguing over which American League shortstop is the best. Some fans like Derek. Others prefer Alex Rodriguez of the Seattle Mariners, Nomar Garciaparra of the Boston Red Sox, or Omar Vizquel of the Cleveland Indians. Derek, Alex, Nomar, and Omar are outstanding all-around players. But Derek stands out because he has done something the other three shortstops haven't done: He has helped lead his team to the World Series championship twice.

"This is a great time for shortstops," says Derek. "There are some really good ones out there now." The Yankees and their fans know they have the best in baseball.

Derek's solid hitting and slick fielding have made him one of the Yankees' most dominant players.

"Derek has a tremendous amount of talent. The sky is the limit for him." — Chuck Knoblauch, New York Yankee second baseman

DEREK FACTS

BORN: June 26, 1974, in Pequannock, New Jersey
HEIGHT: 6' 3"
WEIGHT: 195 pounds
ENTERED MAJORS: 1996

CAREER HIGHLIGHTS

• Owns the record for most runs scored by a shortstop (352) in his first three big-league seasons
• Was named the 1996 American League Rookie of the Year
• Played in two All-Star Games, 1998 and 1999.

CURT SCHILLING

Pitcher, Philadelphia Phillies

Curt Schilling traveled a lot before he found a home with the Philadelphia Phillies. He was drafted by the Boston Red Sox in 1986. In 1988, while he was still pitching in the minor leagues, he was traded to the Baltimore Orioles. The Orioles sent Curt to the Houston Astros three seasons later. Then, after just one season with the Astros, he was dealt to the Phillies!

Philadelphia must have agreed with Curt because the big, hard-throwing righty soon became a star. He won 14 games in 1992, then went 16–7 the next season to help lift the Phillies into the World Series. Baseball fans got a good look at what he could do in the Series when he shut down the Toronto Blue Jays, 2–0, with a powerful performance in Game 5.

Unfortunately for the Phillies, the Jays went on to win that Series — and Curt went on to battle arm injuries over the next three seasons. In 1997, though, Curt returned to form. He made the All-Star team and finished the season 17–11, with a 2.97 earned run average.

Curt was an All-Star again in 1998. Many people thought that the Phillies would trade him after the season because the team was struggling. But the Phillies hung on to Curt.

"It seems like for the last two years I've always been talking about going to another team," Curt said during the 1999 season. "This year, I don't have to. I like being with the Phillies."

Curt was the National League's starting pitcher in the 1999 All-Star Game. The game was played at Fenway Park, home of the Red Sox — the team that had drafted Curt 13 years earlier. Curt never got to pitch at Fenway for the Red Sox, but he doesn't think much about it.

"That was a long time ago," he says. "I like to think about the Phillies."

CURT FACTS

BORN: **November 14, 1966, in Anchorage, Alaska**
HEIGHT: **6' 4"**
WEIGHT: **230 pounds**
ENTERED MAJORS: **1988**

CAREER HIGHLIGHTS

• Became only the fifth major league pitcher to strike out 300 or more batters two seasons in a row. He struck out 319 in 1997 and 300 in 1998.

• His 319 strikeouts in 1997 were the most ever by a N.L. right-handed pitcher.

"When Curt pitches, it doesn't matter who we play. We feel like we're going to win." — Terry Francona, Philadelphia Phillies manager

In 1998, Curt led the majors with 15 complete games.

BARRY BONDS

Leftfielder, San Francisco Giants

Barry's abilities to hit homers and steal bases make him a double threat.

BARRY FACTS

BORN: July 24, 1964, in Riverside, California
HEIGHT: 6' 2"
WEIGHT: 210 pounds
ENTERED MAJORS: 1986

CAREER HIGHLIGHTS

• Together with his dad, Bobby, he holds the all-time major league record for home runs by a father and son. They have more than 750 homers between them!

• Named Most Valuable Player three times (1990, 1992, and 1993).

W hen Barry Bonds was 4, his mother took him and his brother Ricky to see their father at work. Where did they go? To a major league baseball park! Their father, Bobby Bonds, was an outfielder for the San Francisco Giants.

Over the next few years, Barry went to many Giant games. He had an extra thrill when he did. Not only did he see his dad, but he also saw his godfather: Willie Mays. Willie was the Giants' star centerfielder and one of the greatest players in baseball history.

Barry wanted to be a baseball player, just like his father and his godfather. And he wanted to play the way they played. So, as Barry grew up, he watched Bobby and Willie carefully.

Bobby was a power hitter who could also run. In 1969, he became only the fourth player in baseball history to have 30 home runs and 30 stolen bases in the same season. One of the other players to do it was . . . Willie Mays! Both Willie and Bobby were terrific defensive outfielders too.

Barry learned well. In 1982, he earned a baseball scholarship to Arizona State University. In 1985, the Pittsburgh Pirates picked him in the first round of the draft. A year later, he was in the big leagues!

Barry plays baseball just like his father and godfather. He hits lots of home runs. He steals bases. He has won seven Gold Glove awards for being a great defensive outfielder. Barry has even hit 30 or more home runs and stolen more than 30 bases in a season five times — just like his dad!

Barry has followed in some big footsteps in his career — but he hasn't had any trouble filling them!

"Barry is so dangerous because he can hit for average and knock any pitch out of the park."
— Greg Maddux, Atlanta Brave pitcher

PEDRO FACTS

BORN: October 25, 1971, in Manoguayabo, Dominican Republic
HEIGHT: 5' 11"
WEIGHT: 170 pounds
ENTERED MAJORS: 1992

CAREER HIGHLIGHTS

• Won the National League Cy Young Award in 1997. He went 17–8 for the Montreal Expos and led the league with an astonishing 1.90 earned run average.
• Was selected to play in four All-Star Games.

"When things go wrong, Pedro doesn't look up at the roof for answers. He's got the answers in himself, in his experience." — Felipe Alou, Montreal Expos manager

Pedro was the winning pitcher and MVP of the 1999 All-Star Game.

MARTINEZ

Pitcher, Boston Red Sox

When the Boston Red Sox acquired Pedro Martinez from the Montreal Expos, in 1997, they knew they were getting a great pitcher. Pedro had just won the National League Cy Young Award.

Pedro isn't just terrific on the field. He's a great person off the field as well. After Pedro signed his $75 million contract with the Red Sox, he paid to have a church, school, day-care center, and baseball diamond built in his hometown in the Dominican Republic. Since arriving in Boston, Pedro has also made many speeches about baseball to children.

What question do kids ask Pedro the most?

He laughs and says, "'Can I have your autograph?' They ask me that every time."

Okay, then, what question do kids ask *after* they ask for an autograph?

"After they have their autograph," Pedro says, "they want to know how a little guy like me can throw the ball so hard."

Most of the best big-league pitchers are tall and powerful. Pedro is only 5' 11" and weighs just 170 pounds. He is still able to throw the ball about 93 miles per hour!

"I don't really know how I throw so hard," he says. "I warm up like everyone else. I guess it's God-given talent and hard work."

Pedro says it also helps that he started playing baseball when he was a young boy. Pedro's older brother Ramon made it to the big leagues, and his younger brother Jesus *[hay-ZOOS]* pitches in the minor leagues. In 1999, Ramon joined Pedro on the Red Sox.

"It adds to the fun when your brother is on the team," Pedro says. "Every time I see him joking in the clubhouse, it reminds me of when we were kids and all we did was play baseball."

15

KEN GRIFFEY, JUNIOR

Centerfielder, Seattle Mariners

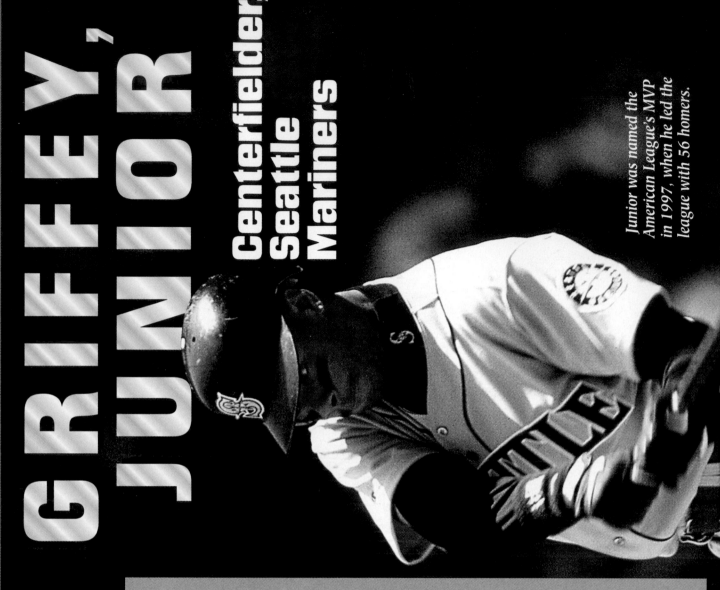

Junior was named the American League's MVP in 1997, when he led the league with 56 homers.

H all of Famer Hank Aaron hit more home runs in his career than anyone in baseball history. He hit 755 from 1954 through 1976. So, which current player does Hammerin' Hank think has the best chance to break his record? Seattle Mariners' super centerfielder, Ken Griffey, Junior.

And what does Junior say about that? "It was an honor that he said that," Junior says.

Junior's major league career has been filled with many honors. He was named to the American League All-Star team 10 times in his first 11 seasons. He earned the American League MVP award in 1997. In 1998, he became the youngest major leaguer to hit 350 home runs and only the third ever to have 140 or more RBIs in a season three years in a row. He also won his ninth straight Gold Glove for fielding in 1998.

And that's the thing he likes to talk about most.

"I take pride in my defense," Junior says. "I can show my emotions on the field when I make a great catch. You can't always do that when you're at bat. And I like to get excited when I make a great catch."

Junior isn't the only one who gets excited about his high-flying catches, which have robbed plenty of sluggers of home runs. Baseball fans go wild when they see that, or when they see him slash a double off the wall or smash a home run out of the park.

That's why Junior received more votes for the 1999 A.L. All-Star team than anyone else that year. The fans vote, and Junior is a huge fan favorite.

Chances are, he will be for years to come. Who knows? He just might prove Hammerin' Hank right. That would be an honor.

"All around, I would say he's the best. This guy was born into the game." — Frank Thomas, Chicago White Sox first baseman

KEN FACTS

BORN: November 21, 1969, in Donora, Pennsylvania
HEIGHT: 6' 3"
WEIGHT: 205 pounds
ENTERED MAJORS: 1989

CAREER HIGHLIGHTS

• Became the youngest player to hit 350 home runs. Junior was only 28 in 1998 when he did it

• Hit 40 or more home runs in six of his first 11 seasons.

Mike uses three pitches to baffle hitters.

"I don't ever expect Mike Mussina to lose."
— Jim Palmer, former Oriole Hall of Fame pitcher

MIKE MUSSINA

Pitcher, Baltimore Orioles

MIKE FACTS

BORN: December 8, 1968, in Williamsport, Pennsylvania
HEIGHT: 6' 2"
WEIGHT: 185 pounds
ENTERED MAJORS: 1991

CAREER HIGHLIGHTS
• Holds the record for most strikeouts in an American League Championship Series (ALCS) game. He struck out 15 Cleveland Indians in Game 3 of the 1997 ALCS.
• Won Gold Glove awards for fielding in 1996, 1997, and 1998.

Mike Mussina plays for the Baltimore Orioles, but Yankee Stadium is still one of his favorite places. Why? Yankee Stadium is where Mike saw his *first* big-league game. Mike still gets excited when he thinks about that day.

"We took a bus to Yankee Stadium," says Mike. "I was ten or eleven. It was a Saturday afternoon."

Mike and his friends watched the Yankees play the Oakland A's. During the game, Mike did some exploring. Before he knew it, he was standing in the very last row of the ballpark.

"I can't remember who won, but I'll never forget that view of the field from the top of the upper deck," Mike says. "The field seemed so far away."

As Mike was taking in that view, did he think he would ever pitch there — or in any other major league stadium? "No, I was too much in awe to think about playing in the big leagues," he says. "I was just a kid from Pennsylvania who was excited about being at his first game."

Imagine how excited Mike must have been a decade later when he *did* find himself pitching in the big leagues! Mike was only 22 years old when he made his debut with the Orioles in 1991. His 2.87 earned-run average that season was the lowest among rookies with 10 or more starts.

Since then, Mike has used a blazing fastball, great change-up, and sharp-breaking knuckle-curveball to become one of the top pitchers in the game. He has won 19 games in a season twice. Entering the 1999 season, Mike had 118 wins and only 59 losses. Later in the season, Mike was selected to play in his fifth All-Star Game.

Now, whenever Mike comes to Yankee Stadium, the fans in the stands are looking down and watching *him*.

MARK McGWIRE

First Baseman, St. Louis Cardinals

"Mark is one of those players who is so special you can't put limits on what he can do."
— Tony La Russa, St. Louis Cardinal manager

Mark lights up ball fields by blasting homers and breaking records.

Chasing records is one of the things that makes baseball fun. And chasing *home-run* records is the most fun of all. So Mark McGwire of the St. Louis Cardinals has been having a great time.

In 1998, Mark made baseball history. He broke the 37-year-old record for most home runs in one season, set by Roger Maris of the New York Yankees. Mark smashed an amazing 70 home runs!

Mark set another major league record in August 1999, when he hit the 500th homer of his career. He smacked the home run in his 5,487th career at-bat — the fewest ever by a major leaguer. He also became the 16th player in baseball history to hit 500 home runs.

"He makes it look easy," said San Diego Padre outfielder Tony Gwynn. Tony was in the field when Mark hit his 500th home run.

But Mark doesn't just hit homers, he *blasts* them. No one has ever hit as many home runs as far as Mark. In 1998, during a game at Busch Stadium, in St. Louis, Mark pounded a home run 545 feet!

Hitting home runs has helped make Mark very popular. Fans from all over the world followed him in 1998, when he and Sammy Sosa of the Chicago Cubs (*see page 4*) staged the Great Home Run Chase.

Mark makes his home runs count — on and off the field. On the field, his home runs help the Cardinals win games. Off the field, his home runs help people learn to read. How? Each time Mark hits a home run, he and Starbucks coffee company team up to give $5,000 to a program that helps teach people how to read.

You could say that for Mark, hitting home runs isn't just fun, it's a good deed!

ROGER CLEMENS

Roger Clemens broke into the major leagues with the Boston Red Sox. He won three Cy Young Awards with them. Then he played with the Toronto Blue Jays. There he won two more Cy Young Awards. But it wasn't until 1999, when Roger was traded to the New York Yankees, that he finally got to play for the team he loved as a boy!

"I was talking with my mother, and she reminded me that I always talked about the Yankees when I was a kid," Roger said. "And now I play for them."

Roger is one of the best pitchers in baseball history. He's a big, strong right-hander who throws hard and strikes out lots of batters. Roger entered the 1999 season ranked 10th in the history of baseball in strikeouts. He also held the major league record for most strikeouts in one nine-inning game, with 20!

In baseball, a strikeout is marked in the scorebook with a *K*. Roger and his wife, Debbie, have four sons. Their names are Koby, Kory, Kacy, and Kody. Roger *likes* Ks!

In 1999, Roger turned to one of his sons for inspiration. Roger had worn number 21 when he played for the Red Sox and the Blue Jays. When he joined the Yankees, outfielder Paul O'Neill was already wearing number 21, so Roger chose a new number, 12.

But Roger did not pitch well during the first part of the 1999 season. He thought wearing another number might help. Koby, who was 12 years old at the time, was wearing number 22 in Little League. That's the number Roger decided to wear on his Yankee uniform!

"We've been talking about it for some time," Roger said at the time. "And, Koby had a really good summer baseball season this year, so I told him I'd do it."

> "Roger has the most incredible desire to win I've ever seen. A lot of guys talk a good game, but he means it." —— Paul Quantrill, Toronto Blue Jay pitcher

Pitcher, New York Yankees

ROGER FACTS

BORN: **August 4, 1962, in Dayton, Ohio**
HEIGHT: **6' 4"**
WEIGHT: **230 pounds**
ENTERED MAJORS: **1984**

CAREER HIGHLIGHTS

• Was named American League MVP in 1986 after going 24–4 for the Boston Red Sox
• Became the first major league pitcher to win five Cy Young Awards. He won the award in 1986, 1987, 1991, 1997, and 1998.

As a boy, Roger loved the Yankees. In 1999, he joined his dream team!

MO VAUGHN

First Baseman, Anaheim Angels

Anaheim Angel slugger Mo Vaughn is a scary-looking fellow, especially at home plate. He is 6' 1" and 245 pounds. His massive arm muscles bulge and his scowling face tenses as he swings the bat. *Crack!* It's another homer!

Mo has been slugging home runs since he was a 12-year-old Little Leaguer. "I hit like 30 home runs in a 13-game season," he recalls. As a major leaguer, he hit more than 30 home runs a season four years in a row, from 1995-1998.

Mo isn't just a slugger. He has also become one of the best *hitters* in baseball. Early in his career, his batting average was in the .200s. In 1998, he finished second in the American League batting with a .337 average. He also hit 40 home runs and drove in 115 runs!

Mo spent eight years with the Boston Red Sox before signing with the Anaheim Angels in November 1999. Mo had some great times with the Red Sox, but the 1995 playoffs was not one of them. He went hitless in 14 at-bats, striking out two times against the Cleveland Indians that year. But Mo grew from that experience.

"I don't think I'll ever close the books on what happened in 1995," Mo says. "I think I'll always refer back to it because I think you're going to learn more from negative things than positive things."

When the Red Sox met the Indians in the 1998 playoffs, it was a different story. Mo hit .412, with two home runs! "You have to learn from your mistakes," he says. "It's not all about talent. It's about thinking about what you're doing, and trying to make yourself a better player."

If Mo makes himself a much better player, he won't be simply scary, he'll be terrifying!

MO FACTS

BORN: December 15, 1967, in Norwalk, Connecticut
HEIGHT: 6' 1"
WEIGHT: 245 pounds
ENTERED MAJORS: 1991

CAREER HIGHLIGHTS

• Named Most Valuable Player of the American League in 1995.

• Has a .304 lifetime batting average.

• Selected to three All-Star teams.

"His baseball talent is obvious, but he also is a bright guy, a no-nonsense guy." — Bill Bavasi, Anaheim Angel general manager

Mo's power swing has earned him a .304 lifetime batting average.

> "Kevin is the most dominant pitcher I've ever played with."
> — Al Leiter, New York Met pitcher
> Al and Kevin were teammates on the 1997 World Champion Florida Marlins

Kevin's steely stare intimidates some of baseball's best hitters.

BROWN

Pitcher, Los Angeles Dodgers

KEVIN FACTS

BORN: March 14, 1965,
in McIntyre, Georgia
HEIGHT: 6' 4"
WEIGHT: 200 pounds
ENTERED MAJORS: 1986

CAREER HIGHLIGHTS

• Struck out 46 batters during the 1998 playoffs to set a major league record for most strikeouts in one post-season
• Threw a no-hitter for the Florida Marlins on June 10, 1997. The Marlins beat the San Francisco Giants, 9–0.

Kevin Brown is one of baseball's most intense pitchers. When he is pitching, he has a *very* serious look on his face. Kevin's wife, Candace, says she can tell by his face when things aren't going his way on the field.

"He gets this look in his eyes and he starts twitching and it's like, 'Uh-oh,' " Candace says.

After 10 big-league seasons with four teams, Kevin signed with the Los Angeles Dodgers before the 1999 season. His first start of the season came on opening day, against the Arizona Diamondbacks. Kevin gave up five runs in 5⅔ innings. The Dodgers still won, 8–6, but Kevin was not pleased with his performance.

"I would have booed myself," he said after the game.

Kevin has always been that way. Of course, he doesn't win games just by being intense. Kevin has great skills, too.

In 1997, Kevin's talents helped the Marlins win a World Series. He won 16 games during the 1997 regular season and then beat the Atlanta Braves twice in the National League Championship Series (NLCS). Florida went on to win the World Series in seven games over the Cleveland Indians.

Kevin joined the Padres before the 1998 season and helped *them* get to the World Series. He won 18 games during the regular season. And once again, Kevin stopped the Braves. He shut out Atlanta in Game 2 of the NLCS. The Padres lost to the New York Yankees in the World Series.

No wonder the Dodgers — and several other teams — were eager to sign Kevin when he became a free agent in 1998. There's nothing better than a pitcher who is intense *and* wins games! There's *nobody* like Kevin Brown.

MIKE PIAZZA

Catcher, New York Mets

Lots of high school baseball players get advice from hitting coaches. But how many have one of the greatest hitters of all time give them batting tips? New York Met catcher Mike Piazza did!

When Mike was 16, Hall-of-Fame slugger Ted Williams came to Mike's house to help him with his hitting. Tommy Lasorda, the former Los Angeles Dodger manager, is a friend of Mike's dad. Tommy heard that Ted was visiting the Piazza's hometown, and he asked Ted to work with Mike. It made a big impression on the young ballplayer.

"It was a life-changing event," says Mike. "It was the first time I thought that I really might get to the big leagues."

Mike still had to struggle to make it to the majors. The Dodgers picked him in the 1988 free-agent draft — only *after* 1,389 other players were picked! Then Mike spent four seasons in the minor leagues.

When Mike finally made it to the Dodgers, he showed them what Ted had noticed years before: He can hit! In 1993, Mike blasted 35 homers — the most ever by a rookie catcher. He was also named Rookie of the Year. Mike has averaged more than 30 home runs and 100 RBIs a season ever since. In 1998, he joined the Mets and helped turn them into one of the best teams in baseball.

During the 1999 season, Mike caught up with Ted Williams again. Ted threw out the first pitch at a Met game. Naturally, Mike caught it. Afterward, Ted told Mike he would one day also be in the Hall of Fame.

"I was honored and flattered when he said it," says Mike, "but I'm not even thinking about that right now."

"He's the best hitter I've ever played with."
— Brett Butler, former Los Angeles Dodger teammate

Mike has hit more than 300 career home runs.

MIKE FACTS

BORN: September 4, 1968, in Norristown, Pennsylvania
HEIGHT: 6' 3"
WEIGHT: 215 pounds
ENTERED MAJORS: 1992

CAREER HIGHLIGHTS

• Hit .362 for the Los Angeles Dodgers in 1997, the highest batting average for a big-league catcher in 61 years

• Named to play in the All-Star Game in each of his first seven seasons.

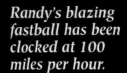
Randy's blazing fastball has been clocked at 100 miles per hour.

RANDY FACTS

BORN: October 10, 1963, in Walnut Creek, California
HEIGHT: 6' 10"
WEIGHT: 230 pounds
ENTERED MAJORS: 1988

CAREER HIGHLIGHTS
• Only Seattle Mariner to win the Cy Young Award. Randy won it in 1995 when he went 18–2 and led the American League with a 2.48 earned run average.
• Led the major leagues in strikeouts in 1998 *and* 1999.

RANDY JOHNSON

Pitcher, Arizona Diamondbacks

"Trying to hit one of Randy's fastballs is like trying to catch a housefly with a pair of chopsticks." — Matt Williams, Arizona Diamondback third baseman

You could say that Arizona Diamondback pitcher Randy Johnson is a slow learner. Some pitchers become stars after only a few seasons in the big leagues. It took Randy a lot longer to become a dominant major league pitcher. He had a good reason: Because Randy throws so hard, it took him many years to learn how to control his pitches. Randy walked a lot of batters. But major league teams were willing to accept that because he struck out even more batters than he walked. Randy's fastball has been clocked at 100 miles per hour!

In 1991, Randy had a 13–10 record for the Seattle Mariners. In 201⅓ innings pitched, he allowed 152 walks — more than any other pitcher in the American League! But he also struck out 228 batters.

The more Randy studied pitching, the more he learned. For one thing, he changed his mechanics so that he landed on the ball of his right foot instead of his heel. In 1993, he went 19–8 and led the American League with 308 strikeouts. He walked only 99 batters in 255⅓ innings! Randy has been a powerhouse ever since 1993.

Before the 1999 season, he moved to the National League when he joined the Diamondbacks. The change didn't slow him down: He led the N.L. in strikeouts in 1999! In fact, for the second straight season, Randy struck out more batters than any pitcher in the major leagues.

Randy's long hair and intimidating scowl make him look terrifying out on the mound. Even though Randy has good control now, hitters are still afraid that they might be hit by one of Randy's fastballs. *Ouch!*

"He'll put you in a slump for weeks," says Colorado Rocky slugger Larry Walker.

Mark McGwire's mighty swing is sure to earn him a spot in the Hall of Fame.

ROB TRINGALI JR./SPORTSCHROME